1   Washing day at Grendon Underwood, *c.*1890

2   *Following page* Benjamin Disraeli stands poised for speech, whilst his wife reads the programme
of events which will follow in this Hughenden Park garden party, *c.*1870

Victorian and Edwardian

BUCKINGHAMSHIRE

from old photographs

Introduction and commentaries by
MARGARET LAWSON
AND IVAN SPARKES

B. T. BATSFORD LTD
LONDON

First published 1976
Text copyright © Margaret Lawson and Ivan Sparkes 1976
ISBN 0 7134 3113 X

Printed by The Anchor Press Ltd, Tiptree
Published by B. T. Batsford Ltd of
4 Fitzhardinge Street, London W1H 0AH

CONTENTS

3   A quiet backwater at Eton in 1909

ACKNOWLEDGEMENTS

We would like to thank the following for their generous help in finding photographs and allowing us to use them in this book: Aberdeen University Library, 124, 156; Beaconsfield and District Historical Society, 92; Bletchley Archaeological and Historical Society, 81, 89, 94, 130; Buckinghamshire County Museum, 66, 101, 120, 122; Buckinghamshire County Record Office, 29, 39, 41, 118; B. Butler, 18; G. Clarke, 161; Cowper and Newton Museum, 79, 125; Miss K. Day, 155; Mrs J. B. Donald, 5, 7, 11, 17, 22, 27, 30, 31, 115, 119, 138; Ronald Goodearl, 10, 24–6, 36, 37, 51, 55, 63, 75, 86, 90, 109, 112, 126, 127, 134, 135, 140–3, 148, 150, 159; R. G. Grace, 68, 154; D. C. T. Graves, 62, 65; High Wycombe Central Library, 33, 52, 56, 71, 80, 82, 100, 113, 151; M. W. Keen, 97; E. Legg, 153; London Transport Executive, 78; Sir Frank Markham, 73, 107, 116; Museum of English Rural Life, Reading, 50, 98, 99; National Monuments Record, 4, 40, 42, 43, 53, 54, 58; Oxford Public Libraries, 2; H. Parrott, 84, 85; Geoffrey Purefoy, 60, 70, 136, 137, 149; Mrs L. J. Stanford, 12; Edward Sweetland, 15, 44, 48, 49, 57, 61, 67, 69, 73, 74, 76, 77, 95, 105, 106, 108, 110, 111, 117, 131, 132, 133, 146, 147; R. Unwin, 9, 20, 45; Sir Ralph Verney, 59, 64, 157, 158; Elliott Viney, 104, 160; T. C. Whitlock, 91, 144; Wolverton and District Archaeological Society, 6, 8, 13, 14, 16, 19, 21, 23, 28, 32, 34, 35, 38, 83, 87, 88, 96, 102, 103, 123, 128, 129; Mrs G. Young, 1.

INTRODUCTION

When Daniel Defoe wrote of his visit to Buckinghamshire in 1724, he commented on the 'vast quantity of beechwood which grows in the woods in Buckinghamshire more plentifully than in any other part of England'. This fact was obviously of importance, for he adds 'the quantity of this brought down from hence is almost incredible, yet so is the county overgrown with beech in these parts that it is bought very reasonably, nor is there likely to be any scarcity of it for time to come'. The picture of the tall slender beech trees, with their leaves turning from yellow to gold, and of the sun shimmering through the upper branches of the forest, is one frequently illustrated. It represents the popular image of the county, and is a view which appears frequently in articles which draw attention to the idyllic life of the chair bodger, making his chair legs in the heart of the woods.

This picture may be found to differ from the reality which appears in the photographs shown here, which reflect many aspects of life in Buckinghamshire during the period 1850 to 1914. The discovery of photography in the 1820's was a turning point in pictorial expression and in the recording of everyday life, for while the early pictures were to some extent artificially posed, there was little leeway for artist's licence in distorting or romanticising the image in front of the camera. While most Regency and Victorian crafts and arts have been revived, it has only been in the past decade that the importance of photography as an art form has been fully appreciated. This is in contrast to the period when it was first discovered, for we find that even Ruskin, that purist with such strong views on art and on industrial growth, commented: 'Among all the mechanical poison that this terrible nineteenth century has poured upon man, it has given us at any rate one antidote – the Daguerreotype.'

The invention of photography was pioneered by Nicéphore Niépce (1765–1833) in 1826 who in time was partnered by Louis Daguerre (1789–1851), a French painter, who in August 1839 perfected the first practical photographic process and patented it, giving it his name. In England Henry Fox Talbot was also working in the same field, and in February 1841 patented the Calotype, a process by which a negative was produced on sensitized paper from which numerous copies could be taken.

From these early beginnings the Kodak box camera appeared in 1888, bringing the art within the reach of the amateur and introducing the snapshot era. But for many years between 1840 and 1880 the use of the term 'art form' for photography was very apt. Just as the Pre-Raphaelites in the field of painting looked at life and nature with a new eye, so the photographers of the period, such as Peter Emerson (1856–1936), Julia Margaret Cameron (1815–1879), David Octavius Hill (1802–1870) and Robert Adamson (1821–1848) looked at everyday things, producing naturalistic views of life in the mid-Victorian era. In the villages and towns an interest in the craft grew, and by 1866 George W. Mee, a shopkeeper in High Street, High Wycombe was advertising in his window, next to the 'Pharoah's serpents – a new sensational toy' that he could offer album portraits at 1d, 2d, 4d and 6d, with over 500 sorts, and that photographs could be copied.

Few evidences of the early days in photography in Buckinghamshire survive, except for occasional family portraits, such as the Verney photographs of Florence Nightingale, or the recent exhibition of photographs at Long Crendon. In the commercial field J. P. Starling established his studio in Frogmore, High Wycombe in 1878 and a contemporary description notes that there was no improvement in the science which he had not fully mastered, and 'his connection is now one of the most extensive and influential in Buckinghamshire'. Starling was joined by Edward Sweetland who set up his own business in 1900, moving to the studio in the High Street in 1905 which is still used by his son. A Camera Club was meeting in Wycombe in the 1890's, while five albums survive, the work of Josiah Stone, a chairmaker and amateur photographer, whose membership of the Wesleyan Chapel meant that few events involving the Chapel went unrecorded between 1890–1905.

One of the best-known names in photography in the Oxfordshire area was Henry Taunt; he made several trips into Buckinghamshire to make negatives for prints to sell in the shops. He made a special visit after the death of Lord Beaconsfield in 1881 in order to produce memento prints of the grave for presentation to the Queen, and for sale in Hughenden. Events such as fairs, local celebrations of jubilees and coronations were often recorded by itinerant photographers, whose ability to capture an eye-catching scene and produce postcards for sale quickly, has enabled us to participate in many of the events of town and village life of a hundred years ago.

The preservation and the copying of these photographs is now taken seriously, and with the help of series in newspapers and the enthusiasm of photographic and historical societies, many have survived. The Wolverton Archaeological Society leads the way in North Buckinghamshire, having a collection of over 6000 slides for an area north of Winslow to Olney. The work was started in 1963–4 and has continued, making slides of old photographs and taking views of threatened buildings as well, to show how the area is changing over the years. Other collections are held by the Bucks Archaeological Society at the County Museum, by Chesham District Council, and by the Museum of English Rural Life at Reading. In High Wycombe the process of discovering prints and copying them is the work of Ronald Goodearl, whose series on Old Wycombe in the Bucks Free Press has brought more photographs to light than any appeals by local bodies. We find the collection of Edward Sweetland dating from 1900 is still in use, with the photographs of bodgers working in the woods, or chairmakers in the factories always in demand by students completing their local studies.

These collections have created a reservoir of prints in which both everyday events and dramatic happenings are recorded. The Sunday School outings were obvious favourites, as parents would be sure to purchase several copies of prints including their family. The dramatic pictures of the troops off to the Boer War, or the Royal Barge on the Thames could be turned into postcards for rapid sale. In all these, the interest in the camera often superseded the interest in the event itself. This is particularly noticeable with the 'elephant' balloon campaign in High Wycombe, where the arrival of the photographer eclipsed much of the interest in the unusual sight itself (132).

An important use of these photographs today is the view they give us of social life as it changed over the years, of parts of the countryside before development covered them with houses and factories, and of the quiet streets of the towns themselves before the motor car brought havoc to their order and safety.

Buckinghamshire in the mid-nineteenth century was mostly rural, and noticeably agricultural. Only two main areas of industry were apparent, the railway shops at Wolverton and the furniture industry in the Chilterns. Several rivers and canals act as boundaries or pass through the county, and at the southernmost boundary the Thames runs through several attractive towns and villages which were frequently alive with pleasure traffic, regattas and college events.

In the 1860's about half of the county consisted of arable land, with a greater part of the Vale of Aylesbury devoted to grazing and dairy farms. Sheep had been raised here for centuries, and it was noted in 1660 that the largest bodied sheep in England were bred here. Aylesbury and its neighbourhood became famous for the rearing of ducks which were ready for the table very early in the Spring, while large quantities of butter were being supplied to the London market.

The labourers were generally engaged in fieldwork, and the pay was low, so they were often supported by the money their wives made producing pillow lace. The low wages continued to the 1880's when eight shillings a week was not unusual; by 1890 they had risen to 13 shillings, but in many areas the help from the women was lost as the lace industry declined. Frequently help was needed, and this could sometimes be supplied from local charities. In Eythorpe an 'alms cow' was kept by the tenants of Lodge Farm, which was milked for the aged poor of Waddesdon.

The outward beauty of Buckinghamshire was of no help or comfort to the hungry, so another charity was spent in assisting poor parishioners to emigrate. At the same time as this decline in the standards of the labourer, an interest in mechanical farming was gathering momentum. In September 1861 a large group of 'influential gentlemen and practical farmers' met at Stony Stratford to watch a trial of steam implements. The highlight of the proceedings was an adjournment to a large workshop nearby 'to which the decorations imparted quite a gay and ball-like appearance; and the whole was lighted with gas made on the premises.'

A love of the countryside was deep rooted in the inhabitants, and Henry Kingsley writes of the 'many delightful varieties of hill and dale; it seems to afford security for retirement, and for those who love to watch the sparkling brooks, and gaze with delight on the verdure and fertility of the surrounding pasture . . . or repose in the shade of the secluded woods'. Many poets are associated with the county, from John Milton (1608–74) residing at Chalfont St Giles and Edmund Waller (1606–87) at Beaconsfield in Stuart times to William Cowper (1731–1800) at Olney and Percy Bysshe Shelley (1792–1822) at Marlow, while Thomas Gray (1716–71) immortalised Stoke Poges in his *Elegy in a Country Churchyard*.

The literary interest of the mid- to late nineteenth century was well supplied at Hughenden. Here lived Benjamin Disraeli, and near by at Bradenham House was the home of his father, Isaac D'Israeli, writer of *The Curiosities of Literature*. Benjamin Disraeli came to Hughenden Manor in 1848, by which time he was an eminent author and noted statesman. Over the period these photographs cover, a number of noted politicians and social lions lived in the county. The wealthy Lord Rothschild was Lord Lieutenant, and he took an active part in local affairs. The Verney family of Claydon house were also prominent in county matters.

4 Aylesbury. Market Square, c. 1862. The White Hart was built in 1814 at the southern end of Market Square. It was pulled down in 1864 to make a space for the Corn Exchange and Market Buildings. Gibbs, in his history of the town, says 'An error was made on the formation of the Market Company by the destruction of the White Hart. It was acknowledged to have been one of the best hostelries out of London.'

In 1861 Lady Verney laid the foundation stone for the new Infirmary at Aylesbury, which was based on the 'most approved principles which science, skill and Christian Benevolence could suggest'. The report of this event notes that Lady Verney is the sister of the 'world-renowned Miss Florence Nightingale' and from the archives of the family we see a photograph of her at Claydon House with her nurses, and again with her sister and brother-in-law in the gardens.

The rôle of benefactor was important in the county, and such a concept enabled the Bucks Cottage Workers' Agency to be established at Olney. It was the result of a need for a body or association to collect and market the cottage lace made by the village women, for at the time many workers were being forced to 'lay aside their pillows' through lack of opportunity to sell their wares. Lace had been a Bucks industry for many centuries, and in the early years it appears that men were chiefly employed, but by the 1790's a great number of women were also making lace. With the arrival of the lacemaking machines in the late eighteenth century, the lace-women were put out of work, but in the southern part of the county they soon found employment in the task of chair caning for the rapidly growing chair industry.

For over a century, men had been working in the woods around High Wycombe, turning chair legs on primitive pole lathes, and sending the legs to London to be made up into chairs. One or two factories had existed in Wycombe in 1790 and as the chair legs were diverted more and more into the town, the number of factories grew to a hundred. According to one authority, over 4000 chair legs were being made each day in the town in 1870, and when the great American evangelists, Moody and Sankey, toured Great Britain in 1873–5, a rush order for 19,200 chairs for use at their meetings was accepted and completed in a few weeks. As steam came into the industry, so the hand-working aspect was reduced. The apprentice and work-man's lot changed and the unions were there to help them in their fight for fair wages and better working conditions. The World War of 1914–18 was necessary before the bondage could be thrown off; it was a sad indictment of the times that a mother could complain of the bad example set by her husband to their twelve-year-old son, when both came home tottering on a Saturday night after finishing work, having drunk a good part of both their wages.

In the northern part of the county a new town had sprung up at Wolverton. Here was an extensive factory for building and repairing the locomotives and carriages of the London and North Western Railway, a workshop system employing some 2300 men and boys. To house them was the new town 'compact and regularly built, consisting of several uniform streets, containing about 250 houses, replete with every convenience'.

Between the extremes of Wycombe and Wolverton the agricultural county nestled, with places such as Beaconsfield and Aylesbury awaiting the twentieth century before they would be more than market towns. Slough itself, later to become the largest and most heavily populated town in the county, was still referred to as a 'long scattered town' with little industry or market facilities to make it important.

As we edge into the Edwardian era, the intermixing of labourer, middle class and gentry had commenced. The lives of the children shown in the photographs indicate how vastly different it was to the depressed state of the earlier years of the Victorian period. The backlash of the workmen was yet to come, with the industrial strikes, lock-outs and riots, and we find that at heart the rural element survived in the county up to the outbreak of the First World War.

Afterwards, when the men returned, all had changed. The rural workman was told that the rôle of the bodger was over, and even the basis of the countryside, the beech tree itself, was in danger. No scientific attempt to cultivate it had been practised over the years, and the foresight of one or two chairmakers was not sufficient to replace the volume of timber used in the preceding half-century. One chairmaster recalls the efforts of his firm: 'Father lived to be eighty-four and I suppose in his lifetime he must have planted at least forty thousand trees, and he cut down five, and they were only small trees.'

The character of the countryside has changed since those Edwardian days, with new industrial areas, growing towns and the introduction of different types of trees. Thomas Campbell (1771–1844) must surely echo our thoughts with his lines from 'The Beech Tree's petition'

> O leave this barren spot to me,
> Spare woodman, spare the beechen tree!

I. G. Sparkes.

5 Wheelwright's yard at Chilton, c.1900

6 Mr Bill Corkett used to take his milk to Winslow Road Station, which was on the Metropolitan branch line between Aylesbury and Verney Junction. This stretch of line was closed in 1936

THE RURAL SCENE

7   A north Buckinghamshire village high street at the turn of the century

8   The Green, Great Horwood, 1907

9   A villager with her water pails talking to the roadman in Nash in 1906

10   This view of Denham village in 1910 typifies the formerly quiet pace of life

11   At the end of April in 1908 north Buckinghamshire was struck by a freak snowstorm which was followed by widespread flooding: Crendon Bridge, overlooking the flooded meadows through which the river Thame runs at the boundary of Buckinghamshire and Oxfordshire

12 An 'Oxford' hay waggon near Shabbington about 1912. This species of waggon, with a rather elegant arch over the rear wheels and often painted yellow, eventually appeared over an area from the Thames to beyond Banbury. It collected a variety of names – Cotswold, Woodstock, South Midland

13 *Below* A horse sale in the Market Square in Winslow about 1900. The horses were brought from Wales

14 *Above* The Blacksmith's Shop in Great Horwood, *c.*1900

15 Milking time in High Wycombe, 1900. The shadows are lengthening as the cows amble slowly along the High Street after a day of grazing on the Rye, the common ground adjacent to Wycombe Abbey

16 Herdsman at Stowe House in 1890, with a bull from the Longhorn herd of cattle which were bred on the estate

17 *Below* Sheep folding in Shabbington fields about 1913

18 The annual Sheep Fair in Buckingham, September 1906. In the background can be seen the Old Gaol, built in 1798 by Lord Cobham for the use of the town when the Summer Assizes were restored to Buckingham

20 Family at Nash in 1907
doing their sheep shearing

19 Washing sheep in the river Washbrook between Great Horwood and Winslow in 1905. One of the washers is using a barrel as protective leg covering

21, 22, 23 Haymaking near the villages of Great Horwood, Long Crendon and Thornborough, 1890, 1899 and 1908

24 A gipsy camp at Hambledon, *c.*1895. Gone are these picturesque caravans, but the gipsy visitors still return, now in brightly shining mobile homes, to the traditional camping places in the county

25 When harvesting took place in the fields of Stokenchurch, beneath the shadow of the village windmill, all the family played a part in the operation. *c.*1900

26   A cheerful pair of gipsies wandering along the country lanes at Chesham, *c.* 1895. String bags were obviously the product being made and sold, and wooden pegs and sprigs of heather were also frequently offered

27 Mrs Nellie Saunders of Long Crendon. She was known to the villagers as Grannie Green because of her knowledge of herbal remedies and her skill in curing warts, ringworm and bad ears. This photograph of her was taken about 1895

VILLAGERS

28 An aged resident of the village of Swanbourne photographed in 1890. When the Royal Commission on Old Age Pensions was hearing evidence in 1894 from an agricultural labourer in that village he told the Commission that until he was about 50 he earned eight shillings a week, though he had subsequently been paid thirteen shillings. When work was an impossibility, outdoor relief 'on the parish' was three shillings for a single person and five shillings for a couple weekly

29 Thomas and Elijah Howlett standing by their grandmother's grave in Cuddington Churchyard in 1895. The son-in-law of Elijah, the smiling brother on the left, wrote a two-volume history, preserved in longhand, of the family from the fourteenth century to the twentieth, which he dedicated to his wife 'the worthy daughter of this long line of Buckinghamshire yeomen'.

30 A party of needlemakers in Long Crendon in 1862. Needle making was started in this village at the end of the sixteenth century, but after varying fortunes it finally began to decline about 1820. At the time this picture was taken Kirby Beard was compelled by high costs – for example, coal had to be brought to Oxford by canal and from there by horses and wagons – to transfer his business to Redditch where cheaper coal and water power were available

31 Emma Sawyer, working at her pillow lace outside her cottage in the fields near Chearsley. *c*.1900

32 Mr French, the Head Market Porter in Winslow advertising a farm sale for George Wigley. The same bell is used by the firm today some ninety years later

33 *Below* A Dame's school in Newlands, High Wycombe, c.1875, with a young child reading to the small class as neighbouring housewives look on with amusement. This area has now gone, replaced only recently by the large shopping area known as 'The Octagon' and the bus station

34 Dr Grace, his two ushers and his pupils outside the School in Winslow in 1890, described as a very respectable boarding academy for young gentlemen

35 James and Susannah Ridge with their family in the garden of Home Farm, Thornborough in 1873

36 A Victorian family group from High Wycombe taken in the back-yard *c*.1890, and then again in the studio of the photographer about eight years later

37 The family has grown up considerably, and father, now a studio photographer himself, takes the portrait as grandfather poses in his place

38 Another family group in 1880 near the Church in Hanslope, a village noted at one time for its lacemaking and conspicuous for its church spire rising more than a hundred and eighty feet from the tower and visible for miles

39 Aylesbury: New Road, *c.*1883. It is now the High Street, a crowded double-yellow-line thoroughfare

AYLESBURY

40 Aylesbury: Market Square, 1897. The clock, which was originally in the turret of the Market House, was lodged in the tower built in the centre of the Square in 1877 with money raised by public subscription. Behind the tower is the County Hall, the design of which is, doubtfully, attributed to Sir John Vanbrugh, though the building was not finished till some time after his death

41 Aylesbury: Kingsbury, *c*. 1883. The Cock Inn, in the centre of the picture, was one of some five or six public houses in this square – the Royal Oak, the Red Lion, the Eagle, the Basket Makers being others

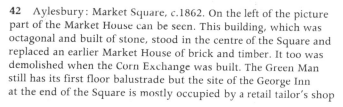

42 Aylesbury: Market Square, c.1862. On the left of the picture part of the Market House can be seen. This building, which was octagonal and built of stone, stood in the centre of the Square and replaced an earlier Market House of brick and timber. It too was demolished when the Corn Exchange was built. The Green Man still has its first floor balustrade but the site of the George Inn at the end of the Square is mostly occupied by a retail tailor's shop

43 Aylesbury: Church Street, c.1890. This street has survived the radical changes which have overtaken much of the town

44 This picture of the flint-covered entrance to the Wycombe Caves in 1900 brings back many memories to residents and visitors. The parties with their candles trod the chalk passages which travel for miles into the high hill of West Wycombe. Many times candles were blown out, and shrieks and outcries went unheeded as the way back to the entrance was sought by scared children. Nowadays electric lights, a taped commentary and costumed groups in the niches help to create an atmosphere, which is nowhere near as real as in those early days. The tunnels and caverns were created in the eighteenth century, and it is unlikely that any of the rumoured orgies and parties actually took place here in these damp and restricting passages

TOWNS

45 Castle Street, Buckingham, c.1908. This street leads to Castle Hill on which the parish church now stands. Signs of the supposed castle were discovered on the hill in 1877 when a builder was digging to lay foundations

46   A feeling of desolation fills the square in Farnham Royal in 1895, as the wagonette stands, waiting for the return to its seats of the gaggle of schoolchildren crowding into the shelter

47 Chesham's Market Square in 1905 showing the brick Market House with its impressive clock, a familiar feature in several south Bucks towns

48 West Wycombe High Street in 1911, with a band of chair-makers straddling the street from the archway of the Church Loft. Careful restoration has allowed the village to show little physical change. It now forms a suitable introduction to West Wycombe House, with its notorious caves and flintstone mausoleum, on the hill above

49 The sloping path of Church Lane, West Wycombe, ambles gently up to the remarkable church on the hill, leaving behind the fifteenth-century Church Loft with its generous archway. This picture of 1911 is little different today, due to the purchase by the Royal Society of many of the village properties in 1929

50 The High Street, Newport Pagnell, 1906. Newport Pagnell, with its prosperous coaching inns, was a staging point for coaches until the railway came to Wolverton in 1840. Now the M1 has a junction there

51 Church Street in Princes Risborough in 1895, showing the carefully tended vine of Vine Cottage, and the rather shabbier façade of the cottages on the right which now house the Branch Library

52 Many of the stories which circulated about the country concerning the West Wycombe Hell-Fire Caves really apply to this Gothic ruin. Medmenham Abbey, on the banks of the Thames, was the meeting place for many of the events celebrated by the 'Knights of Wycombe' headed by Lord Dashwood. This photograph was taken *c*.1895

53 The Baptist Meeting House, Olney, *c*.1855: This was originally built in 1694 on the site of Joseph Kent's Barn, which had been licensed for Presbyterian meetings in 1672. Nonconformity has always been strong in Olney and the Meeting House was enlarged in 1763

54 All Saints Church, Marlow was built on the site of an older church on the banks of the Thames in 1834. This view across the Chancel, taken in 1877, shows to advantage the church's wide spaciousness

55 Amersham Workhouse, which was erected in 1838 and catered for 350 inmates, is shown here in 1895 with the Matron and Superintendent standing each side of the main entrance. It must have presented to the poor of the parish a formidable sight. Now, softened by age and with many later extensions, it serves an equally important service as the hospital for this growing area

56 Lord and Lady Carrington in their robes for the Coronation of King Edward VII (1902), at which Lord Carrington carried St Edward's Staff. The family lived at Wycombe Abbey in the nineteenth century and played an active part in local politics. With them as page-boy is their son, the Viscount of Wendover, who died of war wounds in 1915

GENTRY

57 A weekend party at Hughenden Manor, formerly the home of Benjamin Disraeli. Sitting in the front row of this imposing group, taken in November 1903, is Princess Christian (looking down at the children)

58 *Left* Gayhurst House is an Elizabethan stone mansion. The east side of the building is flanked by a yew hedge broken at intervals by moulded stone posts with open work finials. The first of these posts with the beginning of the yew hedge can be seen in this photograph, which was taken between 1880 and 1890

59 *Above* Posed in the grounds of Claydon House *c.* 1890: Lady Verney, her sister Florence Nightingale and Sir Harry Verney. After the Crimean War Florence Nightingale spent much of her life at Claydon House with her invalid sister. Sir Harry helped her in her long struggle to improve hospital conditions

60 *Right* Children of the Purefoy-Fitzgerald family at Shalstone Manor in 1868

61 This view of the portico of West Wycombe Park in 1895 with its plastered ceiling, plaster busts and shrubbery is made even more real by the row of Windsor chairs laid out in position for a pleasant sit-down, shaded from the sun

HOUSES

62 A bedroom in Dorton House, which is now a preparatory school for boys. The house dates from 1626 though it has been much restored at later periods. The picture was taken in the early 'eighties

63 A view of an upper middle class 'parlour' in the High Wycombe of the 1890's. The remarkable clutter of ornaments and pictures, with the fireside screens jostling the piano, small tables and the aspidistra, is completely in keeping with our vision of what it shoud be.

64 Florence Nightingale's sitting room at Claydon House about 1880

65 Another room at Dorton House, with Victorian furniture below a very much earlier ceiling (c.1880–1885)

66   Horse Bus, Chesham to Berkhampstead, *c*.1880. It was advertised as 'Conveyance to London. The Chesham and Berkhampstead Omnibus from the Nag's Head daily at 7.40 a.m., 9.45 a.m. and 4.5 p.m.; returning on arrival of 8.42 a.m., 11.13 a.m. and 6.33 p.m. trains. (Sundays excepted)'

TRAVELLING AROUND

67 On the way from West Wycombe to Loudwater in 1913, the horse bus stopped in Wycombe to pick up and drop passengers. Currently running at the Town Hall was the 'Yeoman of the Guard'

68 The donkey carrier who ran a delivery service between Aylesbury and Aston Clinton, *c*.1890. In many villages the carriers continued their business well into the first decade of the next century

69 Walter Skull in 1870 was one of the prominent chair-masters of the Wycombe industrial scene. Here, enjoying the pleasure of his own carriage with a favourite dog, he sits outside the two-storey wooden building, so typical of the nineteenth-century workshops of the Chilterns

70 The lady of the manor at Shalstone in her pony phaeton, c.1890

71 The suspension bridge across the Thames at Marlow was originally built in the years between 1829–1831; by 1875 the familiar re-surfacing was taking place, restoring the work of the builder, W. Tierney Clark of Bristol

72 In 1887 the Wolverton, Stony Stratford and District Light Railway started to run a steam tram service from Stony Stratford to Wolverton. Two engines, four cars for passengers and four trucks – two of which had convertible wheels and could be pulled by horses – comprised the rolling stock. Here in the 1890's the engine is off the rails in Wolverton

73 The horse bus was one of the popular means of transport at the end of the nineteenth century and into the beginning of the twentieth. To ride on top, after climbing the swaying curved steps, holding on to the insubstantial handrail, could be a frightening experience. This particular vehicle plied along the road from West Wycombe on to Loudwater; it is shown here outside the Black Boy in 1913

74   The first motor bus in Wycombe ran, as did the horse bus earlier, from West Wycombe through to Beaconsfield. Edward Sweetland, photographer, posed this view of the new vehicle at West Wycombe in June 1908, making sure his poster was well to the fore

76 The firm of Davenport Vernon of High Wycombe can look back with pride at their garage of 1907. This fine array of motor vehicles illustrates the wide range of its activities some seventy years ago

75 It was a sad moment in the life of this veteran car when it crashed into the bank near 'The Pedestal' at West Wycombe in 1905. This was an early date for a motor car accident, and it obviously drew much attention

77 A mixture of alarm and amusement is apparent in the faces of the spectators as King George's motor car swerved to miss a dog during his visit to Wycombe just before the First World War

80 A peaceful stretch of the Thames at Cliveden, where the ferry crossed the river: a view taken in 1908 showing the river boats in the background

78   Part of the first train at Chesham in 1889, with the crowds
lining the banks behind. On this first journey, the train carried a
number of railway and civic personalities, who later attended a
banquet in Chesham

79   Waiting for the train from
Northampton at Olney Station
on the Northampton to Bedford
Branch of the Midland Railway,
c.1900

TRADES AND PROFESSIONS

81 *Left* Mr William Ebenezer Curtis, Tailor, of Fenny Stratford, standing in his shop doorway, 1908. He had been in business since 1877. The photographer with his paraphernalia is reflected in the shop window

82 The sound of the bell of J. Herbert, the muffin man of Wycombe, was a welcome sound on a cold day in 1900. The family had continued in the trade for three generations, passing the business, the bell and tray from father to son

83 Eady's Butcher's Shop at 39 Church Street, Wolverton in 1898. The building is still there and the name is legible, but there is no meat and the windows are broken

84 Butcher's Shop in Aylesbury, *c.*1890

85 Butcher's Box cart, *c.*1910

86 George Wooster was an itinerant pedlar of bread loaves and rolls which he sold to the factory workers in the chairmaking workshops of High Wycombe (*c.*1895)

87 Confectioner's shop in the High Street, Winslow, *c*.1905. Mr Benbow, standing in the doorway, used to write rhyming advertisements for his goods and distribute them as printed handbills.

What ho! What ho! Just stop,
   just stop
And have a look at Benbow's
   shop.
Cakes there are in great array
Just suited for the present day.
Cakes for Christmas and
   New Year.

88 The village shop in Thornborough kept by Sarah Brooks, 1907

89 The bread delivery in Fenny Stratford, c.1906. The Co-op was the Fenny Stratford Industrial
Co-operative Society established in 1886

90 *Left* Prams of all types bedeck the frontage of the shop of C. J. Doel of West Wycombe Road, in High Wycombe, c.1902 The flags and the frequent 'E' in the indistinct sign above indicate that this was decoration for the coronation celebrations of Edward VII

91 *Above* Gents Outfitters in Bridge Street, Buckingham, c. 1906. These premises housed the same sort of trade till a couple of years ago

92 *Right* Grocer's shop owned by G. Lawrence on the present site of 141 London Road, Beaconsfield. Mr Lawrence is standing in front with his horse and carriage. This photograph is believed to date from the 1840s

93 Staff outside the Post Office in Stony Stratford, *c.*1908. Sitting on the hampers are two telegraph boys

94 The crew and apparatus of the Newton Longville Fire Brigade, *c.*1895

95 Two horse-power was the maximum speed the Wycombe Volunteer Fire Brigade could muster when racing to a fire in 1890. The horses had to be unleashed from their farm vehicle and the men working around had to rush to the station before much action could take place

96 The Blacksmith's shop in the railway works at Wolverton, 1910. Originally the works, opened in 1838 by the London and Birmingham Railway, built engines only and employed about 400 men. Thirty years later the works had been converted for carriage building and the employees numbered about 2400

INDUSTRIES

97 The cane was brought from the Oxfordshire–Buckinghamshire borders by men such as Harry Towerton, shown here with a horse and cart loaded up high with rushes, bringing them into Wycombe in 1880

98 Caning chairs was very much a cottage industry in the Chilterns in the late nineteenth century, and this carried over into the early years of the twentieth. Up to the 1930's many children picked up chair-seats and cane from factories on their way home from school, in order that parents could cane the seats ready to be taken back in the morning on the way to school

99 Women worked in the fields stripping willow fronds to make the clean white cane necessary for seating the better chairs. *c.*1900

100 This print of Mrs Dobbins' lace school at Stokenchurch in 1860 shows the early age at which this craft was taught. With her lace pillow and rows of bobbins, each child later kept alive a rural craft for which Bucks was famed

101 Three women lacemaking outside a cottage in Speen. Pillow lacemaking was probably introduced into England in the fifteenth century by Flemish refugees escaping from religious persecution. In the first instance the industry in Buckinghamshire was established in Newport Pagnell and Olney, but with the increasing demands of fashion it spread over the county. The advent of machine-made lace had destroyed the industry by the late nineteenth century, but women continued to make and market their own lace

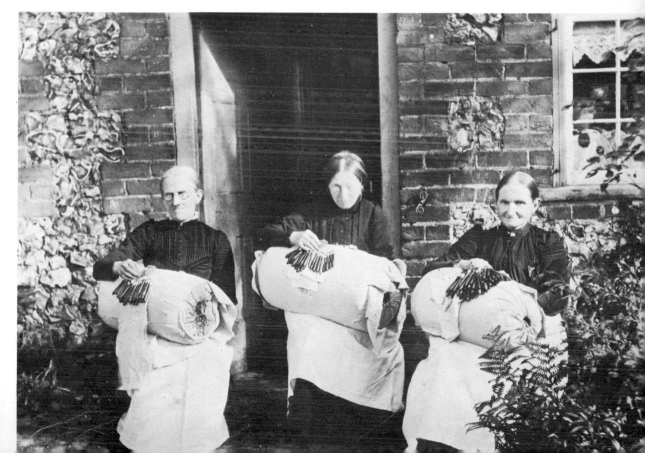

102 The engineers shop at McCorquodale's Printing Works, Wolverton, c.1900

103 The binding department of McCorquodale's Printing Works in Wolverton, c.1900. The firm, which had previously been responsible for the printing of Bradshaw's railway time-table and for the posters in railway stations opened the works in Wolverton and employed the womenfolk of the rail workmen

104   An employee of Hazell, Watson and Viney, Printers and Binders, Aylesbury, laying 18 carat gold leaf on cloth cases before blocking (*c*.1902). When the firm was started in 1867 working hours were 6.0 a.m.–7.0 p.m. on weekdays and 6.00 a.m.–4.00 p.m. on Saturdays. By the beginning of the twentieth century the working week was fifty-one hours

105 Working among the beeches, the Chiltern bodgers cut their timbers, chopped the rough legs and then turned them on the pole-lathe in the brushwood hut. The rough billets can be seen in the foreground, with the finished legs stacked to dry in the background. 1908

106 The pole-lathe had been in use in the Bucks forests for many years, even centuries; although it looks a very rough tool, it allowed the bodger a very fine degree of accuracy, enabling him to turn over 400 chair parts a week. 1890

107 Boat building at Stony Stratford, c.1904. In 1840 Edward Hayes set up in business as an agricultural engineer, but by the end of the century the firm was producing ocean-going craft. The vessels were launched sideways on to the canal at Old Stratford. This picture shows tugs being constructed. In 1920 Edward Hayes junior died and the site was acquired by a garage

108 The saw-pit, *c.*1905, where planks were sawed long after the steam saw was in action. The topman guides the saw blade, and the pitman, whose head just shows below the timber, returns this seven foot saw back to the 'up' position

109 Plumridge's sawmill in Desborough Road, High Wycombe, was one of the first to mechanise by use of steam in their mills and workshops. The large workforce, shown here in 1895, enjoy a brief respite with the photographer before returning to work

110 The sight of a procession of loaded-up chair waggons was a familiar one in the evening at Wycombe, as the horses plodded their familiar route to London, the drivers dozing unheedingly among the straw-packed chairs. This was Glenister's waggon, *c*.1895

111 Whenever any special event was to take place in High Wycombe, a Civic Arch of chairs was erected somewhere in the town. This particular one was built between the Guildhall and the houses across the High Street to celebrate, in 1880, the visit of the Prince of Wales (later Edward VII) to Hughenden Manor, the home of Benjamin Disraeli

112 The arrival of this steam engine at Wycombe in 1893 to pull the waggons of chairs to London created much excitement. Even more dramatic, however, was the moment in 1899 when it attempted to cross one of the bridges over the River Wye and slowly sank through the bridge into the river itself

113   The importance of the paper-making industry in Wycombe is often overshadowed by the chair making. This venerable picture of T. B. Ford, one of the foremost characters of the nineteenth century, was taken about 1865–70. His firm were manufacturers of blotting paper in Loudwater, and were one of the larger mills of the many which dotted the banks of the River Wye in its journey through the Wycombe Valley. It offered considerable employment for the workmen both before and during the expansion of other industries in the town

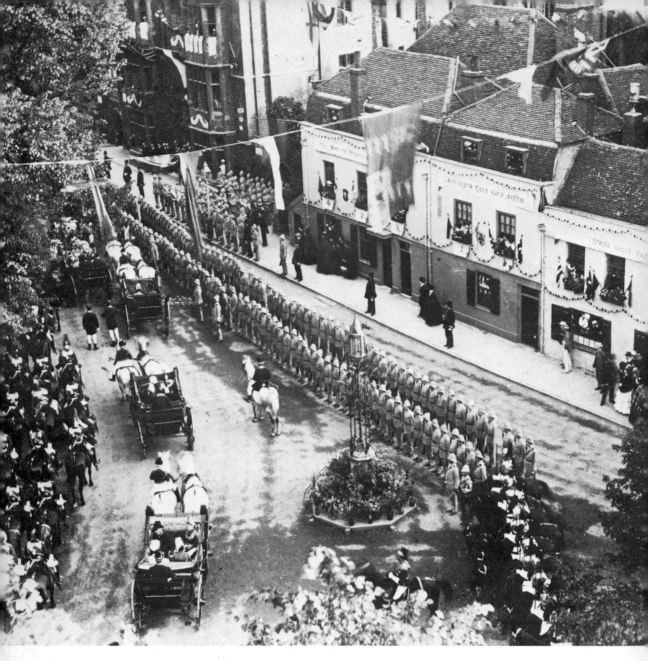

114   The royal carriage of Queen Victoria passing through the streets of Eton, 22 June 1887

NOTABLE EVENTS

115   A village wedding in Chilton, *c*.1910

116 A wedding in Stony Stratford, 1898. The motor car is a
Daimler with bodywork made by Salmons of Newport Pagnell

117 When the Rev. R. Oakley,
Vicar of Wycombe, was killed
in a motor-cycle accident in
1905, a civic funeral was
arranged. Here in the procession
we see the flower-bedecked fire
engine, followed by the coffin
being led slowly along the
banks of the Wye by the Fire
Chief who walks solemnly in
front

118 The Comte de Paris, grandson of Louis Philippe and heir to the throne of France, lying in state in the Marble Hall of Stowe House. After the death of the second Duke of Buckingham in 1889 the house and estate were let to the Comte de Paris, who died there in 1894

119 Visitors at a Church fête, *c.*1902

120 Coronation Tea in the Town Hall, Aylesbury, 22 June 1911. The children had attended a ceremony for the laying of the foundation stone of the pedestal for the statue of John Hampden in the Market Square, where they had sung the National Anthem, Land of Hope and Glory and God Bless the Prince of Wales, accompanied by the Printing Works Band. Each child was presented with a coronation souvenir mug

121 The royal barge on the Thames at Eton 13 June 1904. Queen Alexandra and King Edward VII can be seen inside, as the barge is rowed into the centre of the river

122   Tea in the High Street at Woburn Sands at a celebration for the coronation of Edward VII in 1902

123   A protest meeting in the Market Square, Winslow over Lloyd George's Bill for the Disestablishment of the Church in Wales, June 1913

124 The Great Marlow Regatta of 1875, a few years before
J. Ashby Storry wrote:
When London's getting hot and dry,
  And half the season's done.
To Marlow you should quickly fly,
  And bask there in the sun.

125 Members of the Cowper and Newton Society outside
William Cowper's house in Olney, which was presented to the
town by W. H. Collingridge on 25 April 1900. On this occasion,
announced a contemporary poster 'there will be a public
celebration'

126 Sunday School Treats were always sunshine days, and these children stand waiting in Wycombe, *c.* 1890, for the waggonettes which will carry them to the pleasures in store at the Daws Hill Park

127 Processions and banners were an important part of church and political life, and perhaps some future suffragettes are parading here on this summer day in High Wycombe. 1905

128 Maypole dancers in the
rectory garden, Great Horwood,
7 July 1908. This was the
occasion of a pageant and gala
day for the visit of missionaries

129 A group of children
May-garlanding on May Day
1906 in Winslow. It was a local
custom for children to make
their garlands of spring flowers
and to sing round the village
in order to collect money or
any other reward. The lines of
doggerel verse, which varied
slightly in different villages,
were not entirely light-hearted.

> A branch of May I have
>   brought you
> And at your door I stand
> Old man, old man your life's
>   a span
> Your flesh is like a flower
> Is here today and gone
>   tomorrow
> And cut down in an hour.
> So God bless you all both
>   great and small
> For I wish you a merry month
>   of May.

130 One of the annual parades of the Amalgamated Society of Railway Servants. These parades were held between 1900 and 1914, usually on Bank Holidays, to raise money for orphans

131 The Wycombe 'Weighing in' ceremony of 1906, when the Mayor, Aldermen and Councillors are all weighed and the figures compared against those of the previous year. When the cry of '. . . and some more' was shouted, a great cry of disapproval went up, as the owner was considered to have grown fat at the expense of the ratepayers. If the cry was 'and no more . . .' then a cheer indicated that the councillor had lost weight in fighting for the rights of his electors

133 A truly Civic outing on the Thames, with the High Wycombe Borough members, officials and wives, supported by the uniformed mace bearers, enjoying a pause at Bray Lock c.1900

132 There was great excitement at the Frogmore Fountain in High Wycombe during the Sunday School Treat of May 1903. This very real elephant was let loose in the air to advertise the merits of Salmon's Teas, but the camera captured almost as much interest from the children in the foreground

134   Vote for Rutland, was the slogan pasted up outside Desborough Road Schools at High Wycombe in 1890, during this rather quiet election campaign

135 The summer outing to Burnham Beeches was considered a special treat. Here, in 1895, we see the whole family clambering on to an ancient beech tree to pose for the family album

LEISURE AND PLEASURE

136 Isabelle, Comtesse de Paris, her daughter Princess Hélène and the Comte de Paris outside Shalstone Manor in 1891. In a letter the Comtesse writes that, if it is agreeable, 'je viendrai "meet" chez vous avec mes chiens'.

137   A party in the grounds of Shalstone Manor, *c.*1890

138   Shooting party near Chearsley, *c.* 1870. Seated in the pony trap is Thomas Hayton, a local vicar from 1821–1887

139 Two young ladies picking flowers at Burnham Beeches, *c.* 1875

140 A moment of peace away from the children during the Wesleyan Sunday School Treat of *c.*1890 at Daws Hill Park, High Wycombe. This most naturally posed photograph shows us the aprons and the child carriages, the bonnets, and the gossip which carried on as the children played their games and ran their races

141 Seated in the garden beside the mechanical waterwheel, these two smartly dressed sons of a chairmaster relax on a Sunday afternoon in the 1890's

142 The High Wycombe Camera Club members pose with their cameras during a days outing to Hughenden Park in 1895

143 A picturesque corner of Monks Risborough, c.1895, as a photographer pauses to adjust his camera

144 Ox Roasting at the fair
in Buckingham on 20 October
1906. On this occasion the
beast had been given by two
farmers and the proceeds were
handed to the 'Nursing Home',
later known as the Cottage
Hospital. It was reported that a
crowd of 2000 persons attended

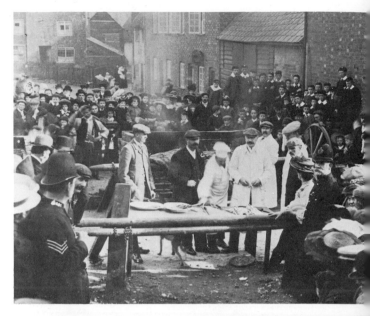

145 The foreign street
musicians, once a familiar sight,
are here wandering down a
street in Taplow Village in
1880

146 Threepence, sixpence and one shilling were the seats at Wycombe 'Palace' in Frogmore in 1910. It still stands, the only remaining cinema in the town, but the prices are somewhat higher nowadays

147 *Above* The Wycombe
Motor-cycle Club waits ready
to start off into the country in
1904

148 The latest models in
cycle transport are on display
at Davenport Vernon's at
Wycombe in 1890

149 Two high-class bicycles in 1900 and their decorously clad riders

150 The Wesleyan Guild Cycle Club, *c.*1895

151 Wycombe Abbey's role as a major girls' public school set in the centre of the town has made for close connection with many of the functions in public and social life. Here we see the lacrosse team of 1909, a reminder of its earlier years in the town

152 Cookham Lock on the River Thames, c.1895. A summer social scene, with parasols and punt poles taking precedence over the normal barge traffic

153 A tennis party at Fenny Stratford Vicarage, c.1890. The vicar is in the foreground

154 Hurdle race over sheep hurdles in the Aston Clinton Sports, 1898

155 Tennis on the court behind the White Hart Inn in Beaconsfield, *c.* 1900

156 Near Wright's Lawn, Great Marlow, *c.*1910

IN DEFENCE OF THE REALM

158 Florence Nightingale, in the window, with the nurses of St Thomas' Hospital on a visit to Claydon House, 1887

159 The Bucks Militia sets out for the Boer War, accompanied along the road by supporters from Wycombe, cheering them on their way

157 *Left* A parade of the Buckingham and Winslow Volunteers in the grounds of Claydon House. This Rifle Corps was formed in 1860 when there was a scare of invasion by Napoleon III. Each man was expected to find his uniform, but the government provided the rifles

160 A group of officers of the Buckinghamshire Rifle Volunteers at their annual camp in 1867. The five local Rifle Volunteer companies, formed in the county, were joined into a battalion in 1863

161 The Royal Bucks Hussars encamped in the grounds of Stowe during their annual yeomanry training in 1910. The south front of the house can be seen in the background